HOW TO TEACH KIDS Empathy

A Parent's Guide to Raising Compassion Humans

ANN HESTER

Copyright © 2024 by Ann Hester

All rights reserved.

No portion of this book may be reproduced in any form without written permission from the publisher or author, except as permitted by U.S. copyright law.

Contents

1. Introduction   1
   Empathy can save the world.

2. Chapter 1 Understanding Empathy   5
   What Is Empathy?
   How Empathy Develops in Childhood
   Signs of an Empathetic Child

3. Chapter 2 Modeling Empathy as a Parent   13
   Modeling Empathy for Children
   Reacting Empathetically to a Child's Emotions
   Non-Empathetic Responses to Avoid

4. Chapter 3 Reading Books to Build Empathy   21
   Selecting Children's Books With Rich Characters and Perspectives
   How to Discuss Emotions of Characters With Children
   Helping Children Connect Stories to Real Life

5. Chapter 4 Cultivating Emotional Identification Skills   29
   Charades and Flashcards: Feelings Activities

Helping Refine a Child's Emotional Vocabulary
Facial Expressions and Body Language

6. Chapter 5 Expressive Empathy — 37
   Setting Up Scenarios
   Taking Turns Playing Roles
   Post-Roleplay Discussion

7. Chapter 6 Promoting Perspective-Taking — 43
   Reflecting on Other Points of View
   Same Event, Different Experience
   Considering the Needs of Others

8. Chapter 7 Inspiring Compassionate Action — 51
   Brainstorming Acts of Kindness
   Promoting Small Acts of Kindness in Daily Life
   Discussing the Ripple Effect of Positive Actions
   Volunteering as a Family: Group Compassion

9. Chapter 8 Conflict Resolution — 59
   Teaching Problem-Solving Skills
   Guiding Children to Resolve Conflicts With Empathy
   Reflecting on How Our Actions Impact Others
   Inclusion and Acceptance: Celebrating Diversity

10. Conclusion — 67

11. References — 69

12. Word by the Author — 73

Bonus — 74

Introduction

EMPATHY CAN SAVE THE WORLD.

Imagine a society filled with people who were taught empathy from childhood. Empathy extends far beyond holding doors for the person behind you and saying "please" and "thank you." Thanks to the power of empathy, children on playgrounds take turns, share, and include others, helping them experience true joy. Individuals with empathy treat others with genuine kindness and compassion. There is absolutely no reason to say that everyone shouldn't be more empathetic.

Empathy involves the unparalleled ability to understand and respond to the emotions of others. Someone with empathy can respond to someone going through a hard time with validation or advice, truly helping them know they aren't alone. As it turns out, empathy is one of the most important skills that a child can learn.

Psychiatrists worldwide explain that the foundations for who we are and how we perceive the world around us begin in childhood. From how we understand relationships to the way we manage our emotions: it all begins in childhood. With that being said, teaching a child empathy is without a doubt the best way to ensure they grow up valuing kindness, compassion, and selflessness. In other words, the work that you do now to instill empathy within your child sets the stage for their lifelong relationship with empathy.

What's more is that empathy can empower your child to overcome some of the common woes of childhood. When we raise a generation of empathetic children, difficult situations such as bullying, alienation, and conflicts can begin to melt away. Children who don't have to worry as much about bullying and alienation are much happier as well.

While it might seem challenging to teach your child empathy at a glance, this handy guide for children ages five to twelve shows you everything you need to foster empathy within a household, impart empathetic wisdom, and raise children who are superheroes at empathy. Specifically, you will discover the following:

- What empathy is and how it develops, giving you greater

insight into how you can help encourage its development.

- Everything you need to know about modeling empathy. As a parent, you are your child's first teacher.

- How what you read to your child can change the empathy game.

- Professional-grade advice for ensuring that your child can identify the emotions of themselves and others and how to respond to them with.

- Guidance for encouraging children to understand the perspectives of others.

And much more.

With this guide in your hands, you don't have to worry about raising a child who shoves others on a playground or grows up to ignore the feelings of others. Instead, you can raise a child who is an expert in empathy and someone to be proud of. At the same time, their relationships, self-awareness, and personalities will flourish as a result.

Without further ado, it's time to dig into the secrets of empathy and how you can impart this age-old skill into your child.

Chapter 1
Understanding Empathy

♥

In order to truly help a child cultivate empathy, it is important for you to know what empathy is. Not only will you need to help teach a child what empathy is, but it helps you form more nuanced and articulate teaching methods along the way. After all, you probably know what empathy is in an abstract sense, but it can be challenging to put empathy and its related concepts into words. After this chapter, you'll be able to explain the ins and outs of empathy like a pro.

What Is Empathy?

Let's start by defining empathy. Empathy describes the ability to understand and share the feelings that someone else experiences. This involves the age-old adage of putting yourself in someone else's shoes, allowing you to see the world from a different perspective while understanding the emotions others are experiencing. When it comes to empathy, there are three different forms to consider:

1. Cognitive empathy: This involves understanding the perspective and emotions of someone else.

2. Emotional empathy: This pertains to the ability of someone to feel the same or similar emotions as someone else.

3. Compassionate empathy: Also called empathetic concern, this combines cognitive and emotional empathy with the desire to help someone suffer less.

Because empathy involves a caring mentality that can prevent someone else from suffering, empathy is often considered to be directly related to compassion, which is when someone is motivated to help someone suffer less due to their experiences. This goes beyond compassionate empathy—a mere desire—and turns it into proactive action. In other words, a compassionate person will not only recognize the emotions and suffering of others and have a desire to fix it, but they will take direct steps to help remedy the suffering. Of course, this is a key skill for anyone to have if they're to become empathetic.

In addition, there are several other skills that relate to empathy and compassion. Those skills include the following:

- Active listening: This means that someone can fully concentrate on, understand, respond to, and remember what goes on in a conversation. Many people shockingly lack the ability to actively listen.

- Non-verbal communication: This is how we express ourselves through body language, expressions, and gestures. Empathetic individuals often excel at understanding non-verbal communication.

- Perspective-taking: This involves the ability one has to see a situation from the perspective of someone else.

Combined, these skills lay the groundwork for an empathetic individual who can socially flourish in the company of others.

How Empathy Develops in

Childhood

Many traits children possess for the duration of their lives develop during childhood, including empathy. But how exactly does the invaluable skill of empathy develop during childhood?

Ability to empathize involves biological factors, environmental factors, and experience. Although each child develops empathy differently, the general timeline for empathy and its development in children is as follows:

- Infancy (0–2 years): Empathy is formed based on the secure attachment of caregivers. During this age, babies learn to connect with their caregivers in a way that lays the foundation for emotional development. Children who lack proper, secure attachment may struggle with emotional development.

- Toddlerhood (2–3 years): Toddlers begin to learn how to recognize and label basic emotions, serving as the early stages of true emotional comprehension.

- Preschool (3–5 years): Two major developments occur during this stage. First, children start imitating the emotions and behaviors of those around them—especially of their caregivers—in order to understand the expression and experience of emotions. Second, children benefit most from roleplay and pretend play, which teach them to handle and understand emotions as well as enhance their ability to express empathy.

- Early childhood (6–8 years): Children begin to form a more intricate understanding of the minds of others. This is often when children understand that people have different thoughts and emotions. It is also when children develop basic skills of emotional regulation.

- Middle childhood (9–12): As their brain continues to develop, children hone the ability to tackle the perspectives of others. They come to understand different viewpoints as well as how others may feel in particular situations. Furthermore, children during this stage expand their understanding of emotions to include a wider range of complex emotions.

Of course, empathy continues to develop after the age of 12, but it is before the age of 12 when what you do matters most. After this age, children play a heavy hand in the development of their own empathy. Also, remember that empathy is not a uniform experience and that it will look a bit different for each child.

Signs of an Empathetic Child

We all know what a child who clearly lacks empathy looks like, and it is not pretty. But what does it look like when a child is a true genius of empathy? Understanding the signs of an empathetic child can empower you to notice when your efforts with your child work as well as when to reward positive changes and incentivize growth. Some signs of empathy in children include the following:

- Sensitivity to the emotions of others: An empathetic child will notice and pay attention to the emotions of people around them. Beyond that, empathetic children will respond to the emotions of others in a curious and appropriate fashion.

- Caring and compassionate behavior: Empathetic children tend to be more willing to offer help to others, be cooperative, share, and otherwise engage peacefully with those around them.

- Verbal expression of empathy: Children with empathy can offer kind and comforting words to others who are upset as a part of their ability to express empathy. Similarly, children can facilitate empathetic communication by listening to others actively and then responding empathetically.

- Understanding of others' perspectives: Children who have high levels of empathy can prove that they see situations from the perspectives of other people while understanding how their own actions might impact the emotions of others.

- Response to the needs of others: Empathetic children are wonderful at being able to comfort others, share, or otherwise respond to the diverse needs of other people.

- Respect for differences: Children with empathy are tolerant of the differences of others and make sure to include those around them—especially individuals who are prone to exclusion.

- Emotional intelligence: Another sign that a child is empathetic is that they understand their own emotions and how they may impact those around them. Moreover, an empathetic child is one who can manage and regulate their own emotions. They also have an understanding of the impact those emotions can have on others.

Empathy is an invaluable skill for children and adults alike. The convenient part about teaching empathy to a child is that they learn from adults around them, which includes you. Now that you have a firm foundation for what empathy is, it is time to explore modeling: a psychologist-approved method for teaching various habits and behaviors to any child.

Chapter 2 Modeling Empathy as a Parent

♥

Modeling is one of the most important skills you are going to learn to better help your child develop empathy. For years now, modeling has been touted as one of the most groundbreaking and effective methods of teaching children how to demonstrate positive habits and skills, and there is a good reason for that! Modeling is provably effective and rather simple to engage with as well. Throughout the course of this chapter, you'll uncover just how you can model skills of empathy to a child (and what to avoid while doing so).

Modeling Empathy for Children

Assuming you are already an empathetic person, the process of modeling empathy to a child is rather simple. Still, there are a few concepts that you need to keep in mind to ensure that these skills stick and are communicated appropriately. Many methods of modeling will be intertwined in the coming chapters, so for now, here are four beginning methods to model empathy:

1. Be mindful of your own behavior. Believe it or not, children are very perceptive. This means that children can pick up on behaviors that you might not even know you participated in, ultimately highlighting the importance of self-awareness. It's vital that you are aware of your own emotions and how they impact those around you, making a point to reflect actively and be proactive in changing behaviors that are not empathetic.

2. Label and discuss emotions. Verbalizing your feelings in front of your child is a phenomenal way to demonstrate how they can identify and communicate their feelings. Furthermore, discussing the emotions of others—such as the emotions of characters—can highlight and improve their understanding of different perspectives.

3. Model active listening. Hands down, the best way to ensure that your child develops a habit of active listening is through modeling. You can do so by giving your child your full attention when they speak. This shows that you respect and value their feelings, setting the stage for them to extend the same care to others. Moreover, you can engage in reflective listening by repeating what your child has said back to them to ensure understanding, which is another habit they should pick up from you.

4. Show compassion and understanding. Lastly, you should demonstrate comforting behaviors and showing validation to your child, allowing them to understand how to engage with behaviors themselves.

When you consistently model empathetic behavior to your child, you serve as a powerful role model they can look up to. Modeling is not just about how you treat others; it is also about how you treat your child.

Reacting Empathetically to a Child's Emotions

It's not all about how you engage with others; treating your child with empathy can help them directly understand the true nature and value of empathy and how to treat others. However, you might find it challenging to understand how to best express empathy toward your child's emotions, so let's explore that idea.

First, it is important to be present as your child verbalizes their emotions, which means you have to demonstrate that you are present. Make sure you are giving your child your full attention and engaging with eye contact. Express non-verbal cues that you are listening as well, such as nodding periodically. Then, take the time to listen reflectively and empathize verbally. You can do this by expressing your understanding or sharing your own feelings where appropriate.

Comforting your child is also important when it comes to helping them master empathy. For example, you can offer physical comfort like hugging or gentle touches. However, if your child is not fond of being hugged during distressing emotions, simply sit close to them to offer support. The goal is to create a safe and supportive environment—one free of judgment and full of trust—so that your child can better understand what an empathetic environment is like.

Additionally, you might have the opportunity to demonstrate compassion by helping your child solve the problem they are experiencing. For example, when you listen to them, you can ask them open-ended questions. Not only does this help you uncover more about the situation, but it encourages your child to come to a solution that satisfies their problem—all while making them feel like you've been a helpful agent in solving their problems. Furthermore, you can take proactive steps to explore solutions together, helping your child understand how to act compassionately toward others as well.

Finally, make sure that you are not invalidating or minimizing their emotions. What may seem small to you can seem like their whole world—both due to their young age and limited emotional resources. Be sure to check back in with them later regarding their emotions as well.

Non-Empathetic Responses to Avoid

Even if you engage with all of the behaviors above, there are still some behaviors you should try to avoid when it comes to being empathetic toward your child and modeling empathy. Non-empathetic behaviors can actually be confused for empathy in your child's mind, preventing them from extending empathy to others in a genuine sense. Some non-empathetic responses you should avoid include the following:

- Dismissiveness: It's important that you avoid downplaying or dismissing your child's emotions, even if they do not make sense to you. Statements like "It is not a big deal," "It does not matter," or "You should not feel [emotion]" are invalidating and prevent true connection with a child's emotions.

- Judgment: Do your best to avoid judging the emotions of your child. Judging them will prevent them from sharing in the future. It also teaches them that emotions are bad and that they themselves are bad for feeling that way. This leads to a lack of emotional intelligence.

- Lack of attention: When your child is sharing emotions with you, do not bury your head in other distractions like a computer or phone. This teaches your child that it is okay to avoid true empathy and instead feign it.

- Sarcasm or ridicule: Avoid employing sarcasm or ridicule when discussing your child's emotions. Negative, cold, or uncaring comments can make a child feel embarrassed when it comes to their emotions. Beyond that, it teaches your child that it is okay to ridicule others.

- Comparisons: Never compare your child's situation to someone else's. One of the worst things you can say is, "So-and-so has it worse because…" This teaches your child to negate emotions unless they are crisis-level, which is not what we want.

- Blaming or shaming: Do not blame a child for their emotions or shame them for what they feel. Instead, it is important to understand their perspective.

- Rushing and interrupting: Do not rush a child to get over their emotions or interrupt them as they share their emotions. Remember that how you treat them creates an unconscious standard for how they should treat those around them.

As you can see, modeling is not all about what you should be doing; it is also about what you should not be doing.

It goes without saying that reading to your child is definitely on the "should" list, which is helpful for more reasons than one. Let's discuss how reading and empathy can intersect.

Chapter 3 Reading Books to Build Empathy

♥

One of the most impactful ways that you as a parent can bond with your child is through reading. Books can transport your child to a world of wonder, but books are far more than fiction. They can also empower your child, helping them to understand unique scenarios, make real-life connections, and navigate the world around them with enhanced complexity. In other words, reading helps children master the art of empathy through relatable stories and examples. So, how can you choose good books for your child, and what should happen during reading time to make empathy apparent?

Selecting Children's Books With Rich Characters and Perspectives

Not every book is going to be a helpful resource to teach your child empathy. It can be a bit challenging to understand what to look for when it comes to books that will truly help your child unlock empathy within their lives. Looking at the cover alone is not enough, nor are Amazon reviews likely to say whether a book teaches empathy specifically. What should you be looking for? Some signs that a book will be beneficial for your child include the following:

- Diverse characters: Look for books that have characters with diverse backgrounds, cultures, and experiences. Books that represent different races, ethnicities, genders, abilities, and family structures can help your child understand others more strongly.

- Complex characters: Books with characters that face challenges, grow, and change throughout the story can be engaging and help your child understand empathy.

- Realism: Good books are going to portray characters realistically, meaning that characters will have both strengths and flaws.

- Inclusive themes: It's always a good idea to explore books with your child that address concepts of inclusivity, tolerance, and acceptance. This helps your child learn to understand the value of such concepts, extending them to their own lives.

In addition, it is a good idea to check the reputation of the author and illustrator. Consider their previous works, credentials, and what makes them a good fit for teaching empathy for your child. Books that have won awards are indicators of a good pick too. For example, the Caldecott Medal, Newbery Medal, or Coretta Scott King Book Awards are among some awards to look out for.

With that being said, you have numerous options for children's books that meet these criteria. Many books from your own childhood are likely to be good candidates, as well as award-winning books at your local library in the kids' section.

How to Discuss Emotions of Characters With Children

In order to help your child take away key facets of a book—including emotional connections and messages—you are going to have to talk to them about the message of the book and discuss the emotions of characters for it to have a lasting impact on your child.

It's important to help your child identify and label the emotions of the characters within their books. You can do so by discussing the perspective of a character or by helping your child relate their emotions to what a character might be feeling. Asking open-ended questions can really help your child understand and work to deduce emotions.

Also, it is vital that you discuss triggers with your child. Try to help them figure out what caused a character to feel a particular emotion and encourage them to consider what might make them feel the same way. This helps boost empathy because it explores *why* someone might have particular emotions, helping your child respect the diverse emotional perspectives of others.

As you are reading a story with your child, you can encourage empathy by discussing how your child might react in a similar situation. What would they do to comfort the character in distress? Furthermore, it can be a good idea to try and brainstorm resolutions before reading the conclusion of the book together.

This helps children learn to be creative, compassionate, and problem-solving.

As you work with your child through reading, it is important to create a safe environment that uses approaches appropriate to the age and development of your child. Engaging in discussions about characters' emotions can make reading a more interactive and meaningful experience for children.

Helping Children Connect Stories to Real Life

In order for your child to gain the most from your efforts—including establishing a life-long habit of showing empathy, they need to be able to connect to the material you are reading to them. By understanding how you can help your child connect written stories to real life, they are more likely to sustain benefits from the books and stories that you read together. Some ways that you can help your child connect stories to real life include the following:

- *Relating it to personal experiences.* You can absolutely encourage your child to draw parallels between events or emotions in a story. Open-ended questions like "Have you ever experienced something similar?" can help your child dig into connections and consider the applications of a story to real life.

- *Exploring the themes and morals of the story.* Discuss with your child what the story is about and what lesson that particular work can teach. Morals are one of the strongest connections between books children read and real life; therefore, diving into the lesson of a book can help your child understand the connection of the book to real life.

- *Acting out the story.* You can help your child act out the story through role-playing and dramatic activities while helping your child further by asking questions about potential character responses. This can empower them to consider how they would react in a similar situation.

- *Connecting to current events.* Help your child learn about the real-life applications of what's going on in the world around them. This can encourage critical thinking within your child—especially when it comes to societal issues pertaining to empathy and inclusion.

Reading is an amazing way to become exposed to relatable instances of empathy that young readers can learn from. But at the same time, you as a parent have to empower them directly through proactive strategies.

With that being said, it is time to move into how you can help your child cultivate emotional identification for life-long success.

Chapter 4
Cultivating Emotional Identification Skills

♥

Not all children intuitively learn how to manage emotions. Some children, for example, group all negative emotions under the umbrella of sadness, when in reality there is far more going on. By helping your child cultivate emotional identification skills, they can better understand the emotions of themselves and others.

Charades and Flashcards: Feelings Activities

Activities and games surrounding feelings can be a fun and effective way to help your child understand and identify them. In general, I recommend charade-based games and flashcards to help your child.

Charades

Emotional charades is an easy and fun game you can play with your child. This can help them express and communicate various feelings. During charades with emotions, each player can take turns either expressing an emotion non-verbally or guessing the emotion. For example, you can make an over-exaggerated grumpy face, and your child has to guess that you are upset, mad, or angry.

It definitely helps if you allow your child to take on both roles: the role of acting and the role of guessing. This helps them understand what emotions look like in other people, which is especially helpful because they learn to pick up on non-verbal communication cues. Allowing them to act out various emotions helps them amp up their emotional expression skills as well.

Flashcards

Flashcard games can be awesome as well, specifically because they are mobile and effective. You can engage with flashcard games in the car, in a restaurant, or even before bed. You can do a few different things with flashcards:

- Write emotions down on one side with a face representing the emotion on the back. Have your child work through the deck, which works both ways; they can guess one side and check their answer on the other.

- Add cues for emotions that your child should express or explain. To kick it up a notch, you can encourage them to explore triggers that may cause the emotion or solutions to the emotion.

    - For example, encourage your child to consider what might make them feel the emotion that is represented by the cue card. If it is anger, ask questions about what would make them feel angry.

    - Then help them brainstorm healthy ways to deal with that emotion and encourage them to practice skills like deep breathing so that they're ready to cope when an emotion occurs.

You can absolutely get creative with flashcards when it comes to helping your child understand emotional expression!

Helping Refine a Child's Emotional Vocabulary

Defining a child's entire emotional vocabulary might seem like a complicated task, but with the right strategies, it can become a simple process. The positive impact of helping your child truly expand their emotional vocabulary is unparalleled. They will be able to discuss and understand emotions in a more nuanced manner, which means that your child will not miss out on valuable opportunities for connection or the display of empathy.

So far, we've already talked about three main ways that can contribute to emotional vocabulary in a child: reading, modeling, and labeling emotions. What else is there? One strategy I highly recommend is to create a feelings chart. On that chart, include a word and facial expression that connects to an emotion. You can even add in a character or two if your child loves to read, helping them associate character development in stories with emotions. Then, branch out more general emotions into more specific ones, like having anger branch out into frustration and disappointment.

This can be a helpful tool for allowing your child to point out their emotions and make connections.

In addition, it is a good idea to explore the intensity of emotions with your child. Children often struggle with distinguishing minor upset from catastrophe, which means that helping your child understand intensity can be a valuable skill. Explore physical and mental signs of emotions and discuss what more intense emotions feel like, introducing a scale of emotions. For example, have your child rate an emotion like happiness one through ten, and explain what other ratings might feel like.

I also recommend validating your child's emotions and celebrating instances of emotional expression. Even a statement as simple as, "Wow, that's a big emotion you expressed; I'm proud of you," can empower a child to feel confident in emotional expression. This positive reinforcement allows them to continue to expand their emotional vocabulary when it comes to themselves and others.

Facial Expressions and Body Language

The last big concept that we have to discuss for this chapter involves facial expressions and body language. Children have to master these skills at a young age; otherwise, their lifelong communication may be doomed. So, how exactly can you help your child identify and understand facial expressions and body language?

Outside of the tactics we've already discussed, there are several things that you can do to help your child become a stellar communicator. You can go about it more subtly, including these strategies:

- Games and roleplay, which will be discussed in detail later on, specifically in Chapter 5.

- Using visual aids, including books and movies, to help your child understand what such non-verbal cues look like.

- Pointing out their own facial expressions and body language when talking about their emotions.

- Exaggerating your own facial expressions and body language slightly, making it easier to notice non-verbal cues.

While also working with more subtle methods, I recommend sitting your child down and having a conversation about non-verbal cues when they are developmentally ready. Most children at around six or seven years old will do well with this conversation. Talk about how sometimes people's faces and bodies indicate additional context to reveal their feelings. Provide them with insight into basic non-verbal cues like knitted eyebrows for worry or balled-up fists for anger.

Once your child develops the ability to understand and identify their emotions, they'll probably need some guidance when it comes to expressing their emotions or understanding the diverse emotional expression of others. That's where we will head now.

> "Empathy grows as we learn."
>
> Alice Miller

Chapter 5 Expressive Empathy

♥

Roleplay games are one of the most impactful ways to help your child understand emotions. Roleplaying really allows your child to step into someone else's life, understanding what they may feel and why. When you roleplay with your child, they come to understand empathy in its truest sense; they hone the ability to "step into someone else's shoes," so to speak. Now, it is time for a look at how you as a parent can facilitate the skill of empathy for your child through roleplay.

Setting Up Scenarios

In order to roleplay with your child, you are going to need to set up scenarios to work through. You can set up scenarios simply by writing them down on note cards and shuffling them, then allowing your child to pick them at random. Next, explain the scenarios and choose who is going to play what role.

With that being said, you might be wondering what scenarios you should be setting up in the first place. Good scenarios are going to be those that relate to your child and what they would go through on a daily basis. Depending on their age, some good scenarios might be as follow:

- Someone on the playground is using your favorite slide, swing, or other piece of equipment. You've asked for a turn, but they refuse. What do you do?

- Your teacher pairs you with a partner for a worksheet, but you do not really like the person. How do you treat them?

- You see someone eating alone at lunch. Other people tell you to avoid them because they are the "weird" kid. How do you respond?

- You noticed someone said something bad about a friend of yours on social media. What steps do you take?

- A friend approached you and said that a joke you made earlier really hurt their feelings. How would you react?

- Someone you love is telling you about a recent fall out with a friend. How do you imagine the rest of your conversation panning out?

Once you have scenarios sorted out, it is time to let the actual roleplaying commence!

Taking Turns Playing Roles

When it comes to allowing roleplay to work its magic with your child, one of the best things you can do is switch roles. For example, let's say you are working with the first scenario mentioned regarding someone who is unwilling to take turns playing on the playground. You and your child should each take a turn playing the person asking for a turn as well as the person refusing to share. This helps your child work through how it feels to be on both sides of the situation, which makes it easier for them to extend empathy toward others, even if they do not necessarily "want" to.

In order to decide who is going to take a turn first, it is best to analyze your child. Let them first play the role that is most relevant to them and their personal characteristics. If you have a child who is bad at sharing, for example, then it might be a good idea to let them take the first turn as someone asking to be shared with. This really helps them understand how they make others feel. Then, when roles are reversed, they have the chance to demonstrate how they may behave differently in the future.

Something a lot of parents are concerned with when it comes to roleplay is a child who has a hard time understanding or feeling confident in a roleplay scenario. While it is good to get your child out of their comfort zone, they might understand the empathetic teachings you offer if you make it more comfortable for them. You can also offer similar roleplay scenarios as writing prompts, storytelling cues, or conflict-resolution conversational prompts.

Taking turns playing roles

Post-Roleplay Discussion

In my opinion, the discussion that takes place after the roleplay is the most valuable component. This is where what your child has learned can really be solidified, empowering them to carry these lessons into everyday life. One the best ways to help a child discuss roleplay is through open-ended questions. You can help your child reflect after roleplay by asking them these types of questions:

- How did you feel while you were playing [role]? How was that different from how you felt while playing [the other role]?

- What is the biggest lesson you've learned from this roleplay?

- If you encounter a situation that's similar in real life, what are you going to do?

- How would you roleplay the situation differently knowing what you know now?

In addition, it can be a good idea to revisit the same scenarios later on. Chances are, even weeks from the last time you roleplayed a situation, your child will have different responses. It can be heavily insightful to see such growth, which can help you understand what your child has integrated into their belief system and what could still use some work.

Roleplay is deeply intertwined with the next skill that we are going to discuss: perspective-taking. Let's find out how you can help your child understand the perspectives of others in a truer sense, taking their teachings from roleplay into the real world.

Chapter 6 Promoting Perspective-Taking

♥

Roleplay is a good start in helping children understand that other people experience the world differently and that our behaviors impact those around us; however, perspective-taking is another strategy that you can utilize to help your child master empathy. Perspective-taking involves the understanding that our perspectives won't always match the perspectives of those around us. To us, it can seem like an event that didn't impact someone at all; to them, it can be life changing. In other words, no one truly knows the intricacies of what goes on within someone else's mind. When you work with perspective-taking, you can teach your child to treat others with this knowledge in mind and gain true empathy.

Reflecting on Other Points of View

Exploring and reflecting on other people's points of view is a strategy that is good for helping your child learn to implement the perspectives of other people into their own life. There are billions of people in the world, and each and every one can have highly contrasting opinions on the very same event. As such, it is good to help your child understand that others have a different point of view regarding the world around them. You can do so by encouraging the following:

- Diverse reading: Choosing books that show children from different backgrounds, cultures, and more can help your child understand the way others perceive the world. It's good to read such materials and then reflect on how characters' opinions might differ from those of your child.

- Cultural exploration: Children do not inherently know that the world contains thousands of cultures and micro-cultures. Introduce stories and customs of different cultures to your child. This helps them understand that because others were brought up differently, they think about things in different ways.

- Age-appropriate film and documentary consumption: There are a lot of films, documentaries, and other visual content that can succinctly explain historical movements, cultures, and more to children. Exploring such media together can help children process cultural and background differences.

Remember that the focus here is on *accepting* these diverse perspectives. Your child does not have to feel like they have to agree or "get it" when it comes to a unique cultural experience. Accepting that others have differing points of view is a major step forward for any child on their path towards becoming more empathetic.

Same Event, Different Experience

In addition to helping your child reflect on the diverse perspectives of those around them, it is important to help them understand that different people perceive the same situation in different ways. It's rather simple to say that to your child—that everyone has different thoughts and emotions about the same thing, but they are going to hit you with the inevitable question of why that is. You can explain that the following influences can shape how one considers the world around them:

- Culture: Each culture around the world considers concepts like gender, religion, family, compassion, and values differently. Explaining this to your child can demonstrate that everyone grows up differently and therefore has different experiences.

- Family: Your child may not know that other kids come from families that do not look like their own, including single-parent households and group homes. This can also play a big role in how a child looks at the world, so be sure that your child is aware of different family dynamics.

- Gender: We live in a society that still enforces gender roles, even in more neutral spaces. Explaining that children of different genders see things differently—without validating toxic gender roles—can boost your child's empathy when it comes to different identities.

- Race: People of different races have different experiences as well. This can stem from societal prejudice, the structure of neighborhoods, and even enforced racial stereotypes. While this might seem like a lot to explain to a child, helping them understand that race can play a role in differing perceptions can improve empathy.

- Age: This is particularly helpful when explaining to your child why you do not agree with some of their choices. Discuss that with age comes experience. You've seen how jumping on the bed, for example, can end badly, which is why you discourage behaviors that may seem "fun" to them.

- Finances: Make your child aware that some children's families have more money than others, while some have less. Be sure to inform them that this does not mean that some families are better; they're just different. And such a difference can mean that the world looks different too.

- Ability: Some children are disabled, but your child might not know what this means. Helping them understand that children have different abilities or needs is an important part of developing empathy in children.

That's just the start. Be sure that your child is aware of differing perspectives when it comes to the world around them, and you will raise an empathetic child who not only understands difference but embraces it. Your child should understand that they themselves have backgrounds that make their perspectives seem different to other kids too.

Considering the Needs of Others

Finally, it is important to help your child understand that not everyone around them is going to have the same needs. In fact, every single person on Earth has different needs in some respect or another. Helping your child to understand the diversity of not just individuals, but their needs, can improve their empathy. In general, your child should know that some people have different needs regarding the following:

- Empathy levels: Some people need to be spoken to in a gentler manner. Tough love or nonchalance does not bode well for certain people. They need empathy in its purest form. For other people, more earnest and honest advice works best.

- Advice vs. validation: Sometimes when people vent, they just need a metaphorical shoulder to cry on; other times, people are looking for advice. Offering the wrong form of help when someone is in need of compassion can make things worse, which is why it is important for your child to understand what someone needs.

- Accommodations: There are a lot of different accommodations that people may need:

- Some people cannot walk, run, or play like others do. Accommodation and inclusion are important to them, however, because they still need opportunities to play.

- Some people have a hard time following along in conversations or sharing how they feel. Mental health diversities like anxiety or autism spectrum disorder can mean that some individuals need a bit more patience during a chat.

- It can be hard for some people to advocate for themselves. Helping out through inclusion and speaking up for others can mean the world to such individuals.

- **Space:** It can be tempting to want to help, but sometimes people just want to be left alone to de-stress, reflect, and unpack. Therefore, it is important that your child understands that they should not force their help or presence on someone going through a hard time.

- **Support:** Not everyone needs the same kind of support. Some people are looking for emotional support, whereas others need financial support, food-based support, or some other kind of support. If your child cannot or does not feel comfortable providing certain support, they should learn how to direct people to avenues that can help them.

- Escape: There are children and even adults who are in abusive or otherwise bad situations. To help your child truly be an agent of empathy, be sure that they are equipped with the knowledge and tools necessary to help a peer get out of these situations.

Perspective-taking begins the stage in your child's empathy education where they can take proactive actions that demonstrate their empathy. However, it is not all about understanding others; empathy involves compassion and a genuine drive to make the lives of others easier. In the next chapter, we focus on how one can promote compassionate action from a child.

Chapter 7 Inspiring Compassionate Action

♥

Part of being empathetic is our ability to act compassionately toward those around us. Without compassionate action, one's empathy is short from being complete and articulate. As we navigate this chapter, you'll unearth some of the most effective ways to inspire compassionate action within your child, including random acts of kindness and family volunteering. This transforms compassion into a family task—one where your child truly understands the ripple effect of kindness. Let's explore how you can inspire compassionate action within your child.

"When you step into the shoes of another, you often end up finding a path to compassion."

Tim Fargo

Brainstorming Acts of Kindness

Sometimes, it is not immediately apparent that we can just do kind things for other people—no reason or motivation required. It's a good idea to start explaining acts of kindness to your child by mentioning that they have no ulterior motive other than to be helpful. There is not just one time or place for acts of kindness because they truly fit in anywhere and at any time. Your child should know and understand right off the bat that compassionate action can take place whenever they feel inspired to do so.

When helping your child consider acts of kindness—random things we do to make the lives of others easier—it is a good idea to involve them in the process of brainstorming simple acts of kindness that do not take away from their time, energy, or life in any significant way (in other words, small acts to get started). You can help them brainstorm ideas like the following:

- *Holding the door open for someone.* This takes only a couple of seconds and detracts nothing from one's life.

Plus, who doesn't find it adorable when a kid holds a door open for them, brightening their day just a little bit?

- *Sharing snacks or lunch.* Some children are not fortunate enough to have an abundance of food. Encouraging your child to share their food can be a great way to help them understand empathy. You can even include extra snacks if you are worried about your child not eating enough due to sharing.

- *Taking turns with toys or playground equipment.* Taking turns can be a fun way for *everyone* to enjoy something, helping your child make new friends in the process. Encouraging them to share as an act of kindness can be wonderful!

- *Complements.* Offering up a simple complement on someone's hair, shoes, or talents can really brighten their day, and it is a very low-effort, high-impact way to engage with compassionate action.

Once your child has a list of compassionate ideas ready to go, it is time to promote their use in everyday life.

Promoting Small Acts of Kindness in Daily Life

If compassion followed us into everyday life, a lot of people would be far happier. It's wise to help your child engage with small acts of kindness every day, and there are two significant ways that you can do this.

First, encourage them to use the items they brainstormed in the last section. Make sure they know that they do not have to actively engage in kindness 24/7, especially if it breaks rules (like complementing someone's clothes while the teacher is talking). It's a good idea to challenge your child to make one or two acts of kindness a daily habit. Each day, challenge them to perform one or two acts of kindness for someone else. At the end of their day, ask them what they did for someone that was kind. No matter how big or small that act may seem, be sure to praise them and let them know how kind and empathetic they are and touch on the benefits of such actions.

Second, you can help promote small acts of kindness in everyday life by modeling acts of kindness. You can hold doors for others, complement people at the store, and otherwise show your child what random acts of kindness look like and the joy that arises in others when shown a random kind act. In fact, it is a good idea to make random acts of kindness a habit even when your child is not watching; this makes you a more empathetic agent, which will certainly trickle down to your child and others!

Remember to let your child know that they do not have to engage in an act of kindness if it is going to harm them or their safety. It might seem nice for them to give someone food or money who is asking for it, for instance, but that's not always safe for children to do. Instead, encourage them to talk with an adult about it or kindly decline doing so. Ensure that your child knows that their safety is more important than kindness in every situation.

Discussing the Ripple Effect of Positive Actions

Children, always curious, ask "why" more times in a day than some adults do in a whole year! Considering this, your child might be wondering why positive actions, empathy, and random acts of kindness are so important. In order to give your child an answer that makes sense to them—one that further encourages acts of kindness—it is a good idea to introduce the ripple effect of kindness.

The ripple effect is used in the context of kind, positive, and empathetic actions. It refers to the idea that one person doing something kind can spread to others. Like tapping your finger on a pool of water—something you can actually show your child to demonstrate, each act of kindness spreads outward and hits more people. A kind action to one person can inspire them to act kindly to another, and before you know it, dozens of people have been touched by this ripple effect.

Now, this might seem like a challenging concept to explain to a child. You can try doing so through a story. Perhaps tell your child a story where a young child just like yours—same age, gender—is using a swing on the playground at school. You can change up the following story to match your needs and ideal lesson:

As Chloe swung higher and higher, feeling like she could touch the sky, another little girl came up to her.

"Wow," the girl said. "I've always been too afraid to use the swings. You are going so high!"

Shocked that the other little girl had never been on a swing, Chloe brought the swing to a stop.

"You should try it! It's my favorite thing to do on the playground. I'll help you swing slowly so you'll be less scared!" Chloe offered, enthusiastic to share her swing as an act of kindness.

The other little girl was excited, too, and hopped on the swing. In a matter of minutes, she was no longer scared, swinging just as high as Chloe was.

"Thank you! I love the swings! My name is Renee," Chloe's new friend stated.

"Yay! I'm so glad! Come and play with me next recess if you want, Renee!" Chloe replied.

Happier than ever, Renee decided that she would share kindness with others like Chloe shared with her. Over the next few days, whenever she saw someone afraid to do something or struggling with confidence, Renee offered to help and boost them up. And that was just the start of the ripple that continued to grow from Chloe's kind act.

It's a simple yet effective story that your child can connect to, but you can change anything about it—including names, genders, activities—to fit your needs and help your child understand the ripple effect.

Volunteering as a Family: Group Compassion

Another way that you can inspire compassionate action for your child and in their life is by taking them along to volunteer as a family. I specifically recommend volunteering at something like a food bank or pantry. This way, your child sees the diverse lives that other people lead. Your child will learn about diverse needs and backgrounds, and they will come to appreciate what they have.

By taking your child to volunteer, you also show that no one is above giving or receiving compassionate action. Taking your child as a family can be a good way to bond while giving back to the community and making a lasting impact. And with the sheer creativity that children have, you may even have a problem-solving genius on your hands, ready to put new ideas into action and improve volunteer networks. You never know!

As you can see, compassionate action is by no means restricted to one or two methods. You and your child have endless ways you can engage with true and unwavering compassionate action, making the world around you a better place and your child far more empathetic.

> "Compassion is the antidote to anger, resentment, and fear."
> Gabrielle Bernstein

Chapter 8 Conflict Resolution

♥

The final skill that you have to inspire within your child for complete and total empathy is conflict resolution. Believe it or not, conflict resolution does not come naturally for most people. It's less of an instinct and more of a learned skill that has to be honed over time. Therefore, helping your child master the different skills that contribute to an overarching ability to resolve conflict is the best way to wrap up your journey with this book. Conflict resolution cements everything your child has learned so far—even if their kind efforts are not met as gently as you'd hope. Let's take a look at how you can empower your child to be a conflict resolution expert.

Teaching Problem-Solving Skills

In order to empower your child to work through conflict, it is necessary to teach them problem-solving skills. Problem-solving skills are a bit abstract; you cannot help your child solve every single problem they may have step-by-step, but you can certainly give them the tools to figure it out on their own. Some problem-solving skills that you can help your child master include the following:

- Creativity: Creativity is one of the most valuable tools that a child can have when it comes to problem solving. Creativity empowers your child to find nuanced and intricate solutions to problems. You can encourage creativity through open-ended questions, prompting certain solutions, and asking your child to think about what characters in their favorite shows might do.

- Open-ended questions: This does not refer to asking your child open-ended questions; rather, you should encourage your child to ask open-ended questions about the situation. Such questions like, "What would happen if...," can help your child understand planning and anticipating outcomes.

- Collaboration and compromise: Not all problems are one-person problems. There are going to be times where your child needs to collaborate or compromise in order to solve problems that involve their peers. Make collaborative problem-solving and compromise a habit within your household, and your child will naturally apply such skills elsewhere.

When you work with these problem-solving skills, be sure to model them in action as well. When you encounter a problem yourself, walk your child through how you are going to solve the problem to help them understand how each skill can be used and what it looks like.

Guiding Children to Resolve Conflicts With Empathy

It's also important that you make conflict resolution a skill that intertwines with empathy. There are several ways that you can do this, but the strongest way is to model you caring about the emotions of others when you solve problems around the house. Subconsciously, your child will pick this habit up and know how to consider the way others will feel in conflict situations. Beyond that, some aspects to consider discussing with your child for empathic conflict resolution include the following:

- *Consideration for the desires of others.* Your child needs to understand that not everyone wants the same outcome. As such, it is important to ask what others involved in a conflict would like.

  - For example, your child might want Tuesdays to be the day her friend group plays cards instead of using the slides, but no one else agrees. This is when compromise and considering the desires of others is necessary.

- *The impact of actions on others.* Even if someone is not directly involved in a conflict, they can still be impacted by the situation. This is something that your child should learn to consider.

  - For example, if your child wants the Uno deck for her friend group every single day, this impacts others in the class who might want to play Uno.

- *Inclusion and kindness.* Your child should make sure that, as they solve problems, others are included and treated with kindness.

- For example, your child decides to play a game with others where everyone braids ribbons into their hair, but one friend already has braided hair that cannot be taken out. A good solution would be to tie it into a bow at the end of a braid or something similar.

Over time, as your child implements skills of problem-solving alongside empathy, they will find it to be a natural habit that they participate in without even thinking.

Reflecting on How Our Actions Impact Others

Regardless of if we mean for them to, our actions impact others. Actions as simple as taking the last box of macaroni and cheese at the store can heavily impact those around us in some way—even if sometimes those impacts are seemingly not our issue. At the same time, it is valuable to instill the idea of reflecting on the impact of our actions within your child.

When your child works to solve problems, ask them how those solutions might impact other members of the household. Encourage them to sit down and brainstorm realistic effects that may result in abruptly going to the store for a snack at 6:00 PM might impact the family. For example:

- Mom and dad cannot have dinner ready on time.

- Brother gets picked up late from soccer practice.

- Baby sister gets woken up from her nap.

Encouraging your child to pick a solution that does not inconvenience or negatively impact others is best.

But it is not enough to just think about these impacts; they have to be considered with empathy. This means that it is a good idea to entangle other skills of empathy within this skill of problem-solving. In other words, help your child understand why they should care about the impact of their actions on others in the first place through the use of other empathy skills.

Inclusion and Acceptance: Celebrating Diversity

The last aspect of helping your child avoid and overcome conflict involves making inclusion and the acceptance of others into norms. Many conflicts can sprout from prejudice and even simple misunderstandings about the culture of others. With that being said, some good ways to help your child celebrate and understand diversity include the following:

- *Discussing history.* With your child, dive into different aspects of history that inform how their peers see the world. Major movements and wars, for example, can be explained to children, helping them to understand that everyone sees and experiences the world differently.

- *Celebrating holidays.* There are numerous holidays and cultural celebrations that are open to everyone. You can include diverse traditions in your own holiday celebrations or visit cultural celebrations in your city.

- *Discovering Food.* Cooking and tasting diverse foods can be a great way to help your child understand people who are different from them. Authentic restaurants are a great option, for example.

- *Examining Clothing.* Take a look at the different clothing that other people wear in different cultures and countries, both due to cultural differences and religion. Understanding such customs will be great for your child when it comes to celebrating diversity.

- *Exploring Religion.* If you have holy sites and holy spaces near you that celebrate other religions, visiting them can be a good opportunity to introduce your child to the differences even within your own community.

- *Learning Languages.* Exploring words and phrases in other languages can impact cultural immersion and the celebration of diversity for your child as well.

That's just the start of how you can help your child explore and understand different cultures and backgrounds. When we understand those around us with more awareness, we can avoid needless hate, conflict, and disagreement, making the world a more empathetic place in the process.

Many children struggle to turn down the overwhelming negative feelings associated with conflict. But now, your child does not have to be one of those many children who struggle with peaceful conflict resolution. With your help, they can be a conflict-resolving superstar in no time!

Conclusion

We have reached the end of our journey together, and I couldn't be prouder of you. Throughout the course of reading this book, you have shown over and over again that you're willing to provide your child with the tools they need to be an empathetic agent within society—something that we are certainly in shortage of.

Throughout the course of this book, you've uncovered not just what empathy is, but more than a dozen skills and tactics that specifically encourage children to be more empathetic—both during childhood and for the rest of their lives.

Even when teaching empathy might seem like a challenge, remember the importance of such a skill. Thanks to empathy, your child has the unparalleled ability to interact with others, form connections, and feel cared for by others who they spread empathy to. Even better, your child will be far more likely to live a long and fulfilling life thanks to the groundwork you set today. Maybe they'll thank you for it in the future!

As we part ways—at least for now—I want to thank you for entrusting me to guide you along this journey. I also want to say the following: job well done! You have taken on the task of encouraging empathy, which is by far one of the most valuable things that you can do as a parent, caregiver, and even educator.

With that being said, what are you waiting for? It's time to help the younger generation cultivate the infallible skills of empathy that will save the world. You have everything it takes!

References

10 activities for teaching young children about emotions. (2021, January 26). Brookes Blog. https://blog.brookespublishing.com/10-activities-for-teaching-young-children-about-emotions/

13 ways to raise a caring and compassionate child. (n.d.). Www.scholastic.com. https://www.scholastic.com/parents/family-life/social-emotional-learning/social-skills-for-kids/13-ways-to-raise-caring-and-compassionate-child.html

16 signs you're naturally good at empathizing with others. (2023, July 6). The Expert Editor. https://experteditor.com.au/blog/signs-youre-naturally-good-at-empathizing-with-others/

Anita. (2023, May 5). *12 essential conflict resolution skills for kids: Tools for peaceful problem solving.* WholeHearted School

Counseling. https://wholeheartedschoolcounseling.com/2023/05/05/12-conflict-resolution-skills-for-kids-helping-children-become-independent-problem-solvers/

Cherry, K. (2023, February 22). *What is empathy?* Verywell Mind. https://www.verywellmind.com/what-is-empathy-2795562

Cullins, A. (2022, October 22). *Key strategies to teach children empathy (sorted by age).* Big Life Journal. https://biglifejournal.com/blogs/blog/key-strategies-teach-children-empathy

Engler, B. (2021, October 12). *Building conflict resolution skills in children.* Connections Academy. https://www.connectionsacademy.com/support/resources/article/building-conflict-resolution-skills-in-children/

Garey, J. (2023, March 28). *Teaching kids how to deal with conflict.* Child Mind Institute. https://childmind.org/article/teaching-kids-how-to-deal-with-conflict/

Harvard Graduate School of Education. (2018, October 13). *Making Caring Common.* Making Caring Common. https://mcc.gse.harvard.edu/resources-for-families/5-tips-cultivating-empathy

How can we best teach kids compassion in education? (+ 21 Activities). (2019, July 4). PositivePsychology.com. https://positivepsychology.com/compassion-for-kids/

Kucirkova, N. (2019). How could children's storybooks promote empathy? A Conceptual Framework Based on Developmental Psychology and Literary Theory. *Frontiers in Psychology, 10*(121). https://doi.org/10.3389/fpsyg.2019.00121

Parlakian, R. (2016, February 1). *How to help your child develop empathy.* Zero to Three. https://www.zerotothree.org/resource/how-to-help-your-child-develop-empathy/

Perspective taking. (n.d.). Www.sociallyskilledkids.com. https://www.sociallyskilledkids.com/perspective-taking

Perspective taking: The social skill you want to be teaching kids. (2021, April 8). WholeChildCounseling. https://www.wholechildcounseling.com/post/perspective-taking-the-social-skill-you-want-to-be-teaching-kids

Silvestro, S. (2018, October 15). *Teaching kids empathy & compassion.* Steve Silvestro, MD. https://www.drstevesilvestro.com/teaching-kids-empathy-and-compassion

Using children's books to teach empathy. (n.d.).

Www.brighthorizons.com.

https://www.brighthorizons.com/resources/Article/empathy-and-young-children

Word by the Author

♥

I f you enjoyed this book, it would be wonderful if you could take a short minute to leave a lovely review on Amazon, as your kind feedback is very appreciated and so very important. Thank you so much for your time.

Scan to leave a review
Thank you for your support!

Bonus

Unlock an extra treat for your kids! Scan this code to access 10 bonus printable journal prompts. Start the discussion about empathy with this special bonus – simply scan and download today!